GO, TEAM, GO!

written and photographed by

HENRY HORENSTEIN

Macmillan Publishing Company   New York   Collier Macmillan Publishers   London

By the same author

Black & White Photography:
A Basic Manual

Beyond Basic Photography:
A Technical Manual

A Dog's Life
(with Pierre Le-Tan)

Spring Training

Special thanks to John Carroll and to Natick
High School, especially Coach Tom Lamb, the
football team, and the cheerleaders. Thanks also
to Porter Gillespie and Lauren Lantos, as well
as Judith Whipple, Cecilia Yung, and Françoise
Bui at Macmillan.

Macmillan Publishing Company
866 Third Avenue, New York, NY 10022
Collier Macmillan Canada, Inc.
First Edition   Printed in the United States of America
10   9   8   7   6   5   4   3   2   1
The text of this book is set in 13 point Bembo.
The illustrations are black-and-white photographs
reproduced in halftone.
Library of Congress Cataloging-in-Publication Data
Horenstein, Henry.
Go, team, go! / written and photographed by
Henry Horenstein.—1st ed.   p.   cm.
Summary: Photographs and text follow a high school foot-
ball team from the first practice of summer to choosing the
final team through the games of the fall season, focusing
on the daily interaction and discipline of the players, their
defeats as well as their victories.
ISBN 0-02-744420-1
1. Natick High School (Natick, Mass.)—Football—Juvenile
literature. [1. Football. 2. Natick High School (Natick,
Mass.)] I. Title.
GV958.N29H67   1988   796.332′62′09744—dc19
88-10019   CIP   AC

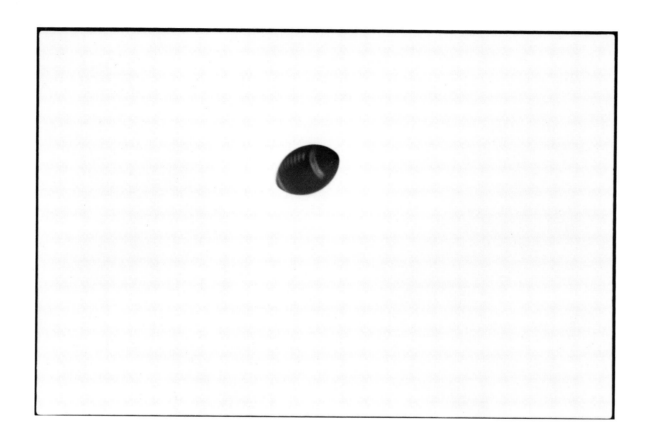

This book is dedicated

to my sisters

Barbara and Ruth

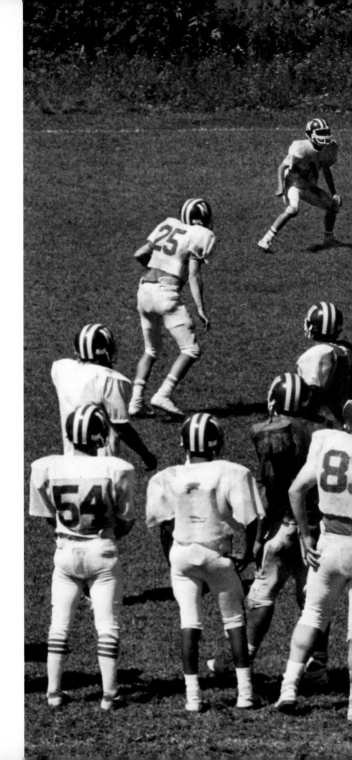

The start of the school year is also the start of a new football season. Every afternoon after class the football team practices. As rookies watch from the sidelines, players returning from last year's Natick High School squad take to the field. Eighty-six players are trying out for the varsity, but only forty-four will make it. Others will be assigned to the junior varsity or freshman teams.

In practice games, every play is important. An outstanding pass may catch a coach's eye and earn a player a spot on the roster. Failure to catch a ball or make a tackle may cost a player a varsity position.

Workouts also sharpen players' skills. At various times during the afternoon, players exercise and run laps around the field. Most prefer playing games, but laps help improve stamina. Running long and hard without tiring is extremely important during games.

Practice is hard work, but it's also fun. Team members are good friends. During rest periods they relax and talk about school, sports, and girls.

There are other ways to prepare for the tough season ahead. Weight training can strengthen muscles, and players with stronger muscles can usually tackle, block, and run better. However, weight training must be carefully controlled. If the muscles become so tight that they are inflexible, a player can become muscle-bound. Then the player slows down or, worse, injures easily.

There's a pep rally before the first game—against Wellesley High School. Cheerleaders decorate the gym with banners, streamers, and signs, and most students at Natick High attend.

Everyone joins in the songs and cheers. The team captains and the coaches give speeches. The whole crowd listens intently to Mr. Carroll, the athletic director.

Because football involves hard physical contact, the trainer, Jeff Stone, is extremely important to the team. If a player has a serious injury, he will see a doctor, but he depends on the trainer's skills for day-to-day care. Before each practice and game, players come for bandaging to strengthen a wrist, an ankle, or an elbow.

After the team suits up, Coach Lamb talks to them about the upcoming game. His job is to motivate them to play their best, so he talks about pride in oneself.

The players respond enthusiastically to Coach Lamb's speech. They scream and yell and gather together with a tremendous desire to play—and win. To perform at their peak, they must keep up this spirit throughout the game.

To help prevent injuries, it's important to warm up before the game. This is true for any sport. Warm-ups help loosen the muscles and add to flexibility.

During the game, the cheerleaders work as hard as the players. They line up and cheer to help get the fans involved in the game. The players on the field can hear the roar of the crowd. Knowing their fans are with them helps keep their spirits high.

At halftime, the players get a breather, but they don't just rest. Coach Kiley goes over what happened in the first half and suggests how to do better in the second. Players are asked what they think went right or wrong and how to handle the other team more effectively.

Meanwhile, on the field, the band gets a chance to show what it can do. Band members must concentrate on the music attached to their instruments, pay attention to the band leader, and march in formation, all at the same time. This requires just as much skill as playing football.

The second half has begun. During a time out, Danny, the team water boy, brings drinks and towels to the players on the field. He loves his job. He gets to know all the players and learn about the sport. Most water boys want to become football players when they are old enough. The experience helps when they are ready to try out for the team.

The first game against Wellesley doesn't end well. During the fourth period, Co-captain Peter is injured and brought to the sidelines. Coach LaCouture asks Peter where it hurts, and the doctor is called. The diagnosis is a bad sprain. Peter will be out for several games—a serious blow to Natick's chances for a championship.

The game the following week against state champion Waltham is a tough one. Players are very serious in the locker room as they suit up. They know they're in for a long, hard night.

The toss of a coin determines who will kick off and who will receive. The coin comes up heads, giving Natick the option. They choose to receive, hoping to score quickly and put their opponents on the defensive early.

Just before the game begins, the band plays "The Star-Spangled Banner." Everyone stands quietly at attention, the referees with their hats over their hearts, the players a little impatient. They are anxious to get going.

After running for the first touchdown of the game, Don gets a much-deserved—and much-needed—break and drink of water. The rest doesn't last long, however. The Natick defense recovers a fumble, and the offense takes the field again.

Co-captain Ken sits frustrated and alone on the bench after twisting his leg on the last play of the third period. The trainer thinks the injury is minor and tapes the leg to protect it from further damage. For tonight Ken is out of action. Tomorrow he will see a doctor.

As expected, the game is hard played. Unfortunately, there are several other injuries. As everyone watches apprehensively, fullback Brendan is carried off the field and taken to the local hospital. X rays show no severe injury, so Brendan will be able to play next week.

The injuries take a toll, and Natick's game goes downhill. Natick is outclassed by an older, more experienced Waltham team. An attempt at first down falls short, and Natick gives up control of the ball.

Losing is hard. This Natick lineman breaks down thinking about the many missed opportunities. Football is an emotional sport. Sometimes it takes tears to deal with the disappointments.

Good sportsmanship is an important part of football. After the final play, the teams line up to congratulate each other on a well-played game. Everyone participates—coaches, cheerleaders, and, of course, players.

Before the next game, against Norwood, the team leaves the field after warm-ups to wait for game time. The cheerleaders line up to greet the players when they rush out again as a group. This is a good way to get everyone psyched to support the team—loudly and clearly.

In the last few minutes of the game, the handoff goes to star tailback Donald, who gets some timely blocks from his teammates and shakes loose for a 33-yard touchdown run. Placekicker Nick has an opportunity to kick the point and tie the game, but he fails and Natick loses, 31 to 30.

On Thanksgiving Day, the Natick team journeys to play South, their traditional rivals. Part of the fun of away games is traveling together by bus. Each group—the players, the cheerleaders, and the band members—has a separate bus. The cheerleaders' is the most active: The girls practice their cheers and make up new ones. They all seem to be having a great time.

There is dead silence in the players' bus. Coach Lamb and Assistant Coach Ghilani sit up front. Team members stare out the windows. It's a time to think and concentrate and consider their roles in the upcoming game. They must stay mentally and spiritually prepared for the effort.

The players' bus arrives at the visitors' field, and Dave is the first to get off. The team will go to the visitors' locker room to put on shoulder pads and helmets and then to the field for warm-ups. The game is two hours away.

A coach from a local college arrives early. He has come to scout Natick's halfback and center and South's fullback and may offer them scholarships if he likes the way they play in this, their final game.

Natick begins the game aggressively with a pass on the very first play. The strategy is somewhat dangerous because South can more likely gain possession of the ball through an interception. However, the bold move takes the South defense by surprise and results in a completed pass and a long gain for Natick.

On the very next play, the cheerleaders groan as Natick fumbles and South recovers. Judging by its start, this game is going to be one with a lot of emotional ups and downs. The Natick fans, however, are with the team, all the way!

The first half ends, and the South band takes the field. Their halftime entertainment includes some fancy baton twirling by their prize-winning drum majorettes.

Meanwhile, in the locker room, Coach Lamb goes over strategy changes,
and then Natick takes the field aggressively.

Natick defenders surround the South receiver, and the pass up the middle is incomplete. For most of the game, the score is close, but then Natick pulls ahead to win, 40 to 24.

When the final buzzer sounds, all the Natick players on the sidelines rush onto the field with tremendous enthusiasm. They haven't won the championship this season, but they have won the Thanksgiving Day game—the one that counts most of all.

The game over, it's possible to think about other things. While the buses stand still until everyone boards, a cheerleader and a player talk about homework and decide what movie to see tonight.

The season has ended, and the awards dinner is held at the Natick Moose Hall. Local supporters and dignitaries toast everyone involved in the season's success. Outstanding players receive trophies in honor of their contributions. A celebration for everyone, the dinner is a great way to close the season. Now it's time to think about an even better season next year.